SO IT DOESN'T HAVE TO BE YOU

Why Me?

So it Doesn't Have to be You.

Blaze

WHY ME?

Unless otherwise noted, all scriptures are taken from the NIV version of the Bible.

This book is based upon a true story. The names have been changed to protect the identity of named individuals.

Why Me? So it Doesn't Have to be You

ISBN: 978-0-578-00395-5

Copyright 2008© by Blaze

Published By: G. Marie WorldWide Ministries Inc.

Aka Kingdom Builders International Movement For Christ Inc.

For more information about Blaze contact:

(516) 608-6712 or kingdombuilders669@yahoo.com

Cover Design: Blaze and Edwin K. Andrews

Photography: Tisha Banks

Editing: Apostle G. Marie Carroll

Printed in the United States of America

All rights reserved under International Copyright Law. No part of this book may be reproduced or transmitted in any form or by any means, electronic or mechanical. Including photocopying, recording, or by any information, storage and retrieval system, without written permission of the Publisher/Author.

SO IT DOESN'T HAVE TO BE YOU

Introduction

Usually, introductions share a piece of what is to come. Yet, I would feel remiss if I didn't do it this way. I was born into more turmoil than should be allowed. I honestly feel like there should be a limit on the amount of inappropriate things that children must feel in the womb... and I was over the limit... enough for 4 or more children. Usually children are a joyous gift from God, people do all sorts of things and spend, spend, spend so that the child arrives into a lavish and lush lifestyle. But what happens when you have a child that's unwanted? Born out of wedlock? The product of rape and an unhealthy previous relationship? Denied from conception? Then you have... me.

What happens when the child can feel the father's unhappiness with her birth? When she knows he would

WHY ME?

adore for her to have never been born? When she's looked at as the mistake? When she grows up feeling as if nobody loves her and nobody will ever love her because after all if her own father does not want her who will? When she ponders everyone's true intent upon befriending her? When she's afraid and alone and feels like nobody understands? When she lives out her childhood and teenage life miserable and depressed because she can't fathom anyone liking her?

    Well, you have a child, becoming a young adult, but stagnated due to circumstances beyond her control. You have… someone who is supposed to be blossoming into an adult and loving life but can't because she hates herself because she's HALF of this man that is supposed to be her father, but he hated the fact that she made him look bad because she was born and he was with another… You have someone who could never ever THINK a man could and would love her, but can't realize it's

SO IT DOESN'T HAVE TO BE YOU

because she doesn't love HERSELF. So she puts a big pretty smile on her face and pretends to love every aspect of her being. She pretends that everything is alright and she's gonna make it and be just fine. But on the inside she's screaming and dying... choking herself, killing herself because she can't possibly be worth ANYTHING to anyone else if she can't even be a GLIMMER of happiness in her father's, the man who should love her the most, eye.

    So what do you have when she realizes all of this and starts to love herself the way she deserves? You have this book, from my heart to yours, hoping you can find a piece of you in it, and learn, the most important part of THIS side of life, is loving YOU... even when you know, the person you wanted to love you most, did not, because of themselves.

    We're an elite few, because so many of us did not make it. Someone

WHY ME?

just like me and like you…dying on the inside, couldn't handle it and didn't make it. And there are some we think will never understand. I want you to know it was US, so it doesn't HAVE to be someone else, and we can keep them from traveling this road.

And when you finish this book, I already want you to know… this girl was ME.

Peace and Blessings

Blaze

SO IT DOESN'T HAVE TO BE YOU

Dedication

I dedicate this book to anyone who has ever been hurt by the ones who should protect you.

I dedicate it to every Daddy's Little Girl, every little girl who made it through in a world where she felt alone, and I dedicate it to the girls who never got a chance to breathe because someone saw fit to take your life.

I dedicate this book to every mother who had to be everything and felt they were nothing.

I dedicate this book to every sister who tried to understand.

WHY ME?

I dedicate this book to every best friend who had sleepless nights and sat there and cried with their hurting friends.

I dedicate it to everyone who can't find themselves and I pray this book helps you, because I found myself in it.

Finding yourself is probably one of the hardest things to do when you're not sure who you are. The most important people in your life are your parents. So when one decides it's alright to pretend you're not his daughter, you tend to be slightly confused. You're searching for the love that SHOULD have been there but never was. So you fight this losing battle between who you REALLY are and who everyone else wants you to be.

Being yourself is the greatest thing you can do for anyone. Never give up on being YOU!

SO IT DOESN'T HAVE TO BE YOU

Acknowledgements

I promise I am not good at this, so if I forget or it's not all you hoped, I apologize. Just know I love you!

Mommy- In my corner from day one, I know God used you to have me. We know the story (and if they want to know, they can get your other book) but I want you know even though I don't show it all the time, I appreciate you and love you, not for what you do, but for becoming who you are. You've inspired me to do greater, and I'm trying. I love you.

My Father- I forgive you. For real! I came to the conclusion long ago that maybe you just didn't know how to love me, and that's ok. One of my favorite films says that forgiveness is moving forward. I hope we can move forward from here.

Randy- You're not here to see this, but I know you'd be proud. Thanks for being everything everyone else was not, and loving me to the end.

WHY ME?

Pop- What can I say? You never say much, but I hear what you do say, and I love you for it.

Rikki- I always call you "MY sister". And you are. I love you for never making me feel inferior in any way and having my back when I didn't know where else to turn. The bond we share means more to me than you know, I love you.

Vikki- I never knew you or met you, but somehow I know I would not be here if it was not for you.

Dionna (D.D)- Being your big sister has brought me some of the proudest moments in my life. No matter what I want you to know I am proud of you and I love you. Though you're not mentioned much in this book, what you represent to me is beyond words. Keep playing Drum Major!

Bobby and Salima- As a brother in law and sister in law, you guys have been nothing but supportive. Bobby making me press and Salima keeping my secrets. I love you both!

SO IT DOESN'T HAVE TO BE YOU

Ny, Q, and CJ- The niece and nephews that God gave me. Ny to eat the mac and cheese, Q to eat everything else, and CJ to ask me for a dollar faithfully. I love you all, and you're all crazy.

Sha- My dancing machine. Keep doing what you do! Auntie's PROUD and she loves you!

Nejla (Nejjie)- You are the epitome of grace. When you're old enough to read I want you to know that I love you and I am going to get you a car, because I can't see you taking the bus!

RJ (Poodah)- My cookie boy. You showed me what unconditional love is. Auntie absolutely loves you, no matter what you do, even when you spill all the cookies on the bed. And when you're old enough to read, I want you to know I will always be there!

Grandparents, Aunts, Uncles, Cousins- I love you.

Kenny- Though you may not always understand me, you were there, and

WHY ME?

sometimes that's all a person needs! I love you.

Cynthia- The woman who taught me to never fear anything. I appreciate your love and support of me from the very beginning. If ever there was a time I needed you, I knew I could count on you. I love you!

Kingdom Builders- Follow the Tabernacle and you'll enter into the presence of His Glory EVERY TIME. I love you all!

E- You stayed up with me for three hours working on this cover and making it what I saw in my mind. I am eternally grateful and I love you.

Mary, Toni, and Sunny- You know who you are and what you've done for me. I love you!

Tres- You may never know how God used you to change my life, but He did and I love you!

SO IT DOESN'T HAVE TO BE YOU

The man behind Cooper- I forgive you too! I even love you, Apostle. Get back on the grind, you'll be successful.

Team Swag- You guys are like family and I love you just that way. Thanks for never judging me. And to the Original Swag, I'm sure if it weren't for you, I would not have been able to dig myself out of the pity pit and live. LOVE YOU!

D- And you know who you are. I love you, and you're truly my brother.

Every person I spoke to on Facebook, Myspace, Xanga, Aim, Yahoo, MSN- The love is THERE. Literally.

There are many other people who I want to thank, but this is going to become a madhouse if I forget someone. There is more to come and I promise I'll try to remember, but if you really want to know how I feel about you, just ask! If you love me, you won't want me to have carpal tunnel typing this all out!

Last but not least is God. The source of my strength, hope, and creativity, the supplier of everything I need. I don't feel

WHY ME?

it necessary to go on and on about You Lord, because this book is for you and because of you and my life is dedicated to you.

SO IT DOESN'T HAVE TO BE YOU

Table of Contents

Prologue

Chapter 1

Chapter 2

Chapter 3

Chapter 4

Chapter 5

Chapter 6

Chapter 7

Chapter 8

Chapter 9

Chapter 10

Chapter 11

Chapter 12

Epilogue

WHY ME?

SO IT DOESN'T HAVE TO BE YOU

Prologue

"Hi Daddy! Merry Christmas!", proclaimed 6 year old Kelis as she jumped into the back of her father's car. It was never a happy occasion to be with her father, but she figured she had better make the best of it. After all, Santa has to bring twice as many presents when your parents are not together. So she put on a big bright smile and went on with her sister Kaila, who was 14 and really did love going to Daddy's house. "Hey girls", Dad responded. And immediately Kaila starts talking about how much she loves Christmas and how the holidays make things seem not so bad. Then she asks, "Daddy, did you get **everything**"? and MAN did she stress everything like there was some sort of secret about Christmas that nobody was telling Kelis. Dad responded "I did what I could do Kay" and Kaila scoffed and rolled her eyes. Dad wasn't living too far, so when they got to the apartment, Kelis patiently waited for Daddy to come get her, and when he did, she and Kaila ran up the

WHY ME?

steps two at a time to get to the apartment Daddy has with his new wife and their little girl, Precious.

Kelis and Kaila didn't like Precious very much. She was a BRAT with a capital T! At two years old she was already driving everyone insane. Kelis and Kaila played the role well. They kissed her and hugged their step-mom, Angelica, and pretended they could stand her. Angelica was no great individual herself. She treated poor Kelis SO BAD. There was never a time when Kelis didn't cry when over there. But it was Christmas, and Kelis new she asked Santa to deliver a bright red Barbie doll car she could ride in, to daddy's house. She was confident it would be there; after all, Santa had NEVER disappointed her at mommy's house. He even went above and beyond the call of duty and got some things that weren't on her list, and he NEVER brought her socks, or something crazy like that.

SO IT DOESN'T HAVE TO BE YOU

So, Kelis runs to the tree and looks for the biggest hugest box... and surprisingly enough, it says that little monsters name on it. So Kelis finds the next to largest box...that says Kaila's name. So, now, we have her sitting there scratching her head trying to figure out where this car is, because none of the rest of these boxes are big enough for the car.

They begin to open presents and Kaila is so excited, because of all the great clothes and games she got, and is just overjoyed with her leather coat. Poor Kelis is more and more disappointed because she's getting Barbie dolls, clothes for the Barbie and all that, but NO CAR... She's losing hope and faith in Santa and wondering how he could play her like that.

Angelica starts to help Precious open her gifts of great big teddy bears and toys and clothes, and she opens the biggest box last. In the box, is a huge

WHY ME?

toy chest. They clean up all the excelsior so they can relax and play with their toys. When they are done, Kaila jumps up and heads for the bathroom upstairs. Angelica says, "We have one more gift for you Precious" and goes into the back. She brings out, none other than the candy apple red Barbie car that Kelis had BEGGED Santa to leave at Daddy's house. So, her throat becomes dry and tears well in her eyes and she asks Dad "well, why didn't Santa bring me one Daddy? You said he'd do it". Her father, Kevin, starts to stutter and Angelica blurts out "There is no such thing as Santa Kelis, DADDY got this for Precious..." Kaila, at the top of the stairs returning, sees the car and turns pale. Kelis looks at her father and says "Well, where's mine Daddy?" He responds "Well, Kelis, I didn't get you one". What a great Christmas. In less than ten minutes Kelis is disappointed by Santa, AND by Daddy. The loss of faith in a parent is mentally and emotionally damaging for a child. As Kelis stood there blocking out everything, she wished she never even KNEW her father. It was too hard to

SO IT DOESN'T HAVE TO BE YOU

comprehend how he could purposely hurt her. Sure it's not a big deal to some, but to a six year old, Christmas is the end all be all of the year. If there is no Santa to look to, then parents are supposed to come through.

With shattered hopes and an anger she had never felt before, Kelis sat at the dinner table, confused, flustered, and silent. Kaila sat next to her glaring at her father and shooting the look of doom at Precious and Angelica. Daddy says solemnly "I'm sorry Kelis". Kelis stares at him with her nose red and tears in her eyes "Sometimes, sorry is not good enough" and returns her eyes to the floor wishing she could disappear. The ONE time her father could have come through for her, he didn't. WHY? What did she do so wrong that she didn't deserve what she asked for? She was doing great in school, always was well behaved and was respectful. Sure, she had hellfire temper, but who didn't at one time or another? Finally Kaila speaks. "Daddy", she starts slowly, "I was just wondering

WHY ME?

what you think you're doing? She is a CHILD and you don't DO these sorts of things. It is so DUMB of you to hurt her this way. We were your daughters first. Kelis doesn't ask you for NOTHING and the ONE time you can do something to make her happy, you screw that up too!"... "And YOU, she continues, now getting loud and angry with Angelica, "You wait until I leave and pull that car out of nowhere like you had to let Kelis see it. What kind of adult are YOU?!?! You knew we were daddy's children and you just come all up in here and treat us like trash? Bringing that car out here like it's not gonna hurt Kelis. You're gonna pay for this, I swear"! Daddy stands up. "That's enough Kaila, you're getting disrespectful," he says evenly. "NO", she yells, "I've had enough of YOU!"

Fuming, Kaila excuses herself and Kelis and calls her mom, where she has a brief conversation that gets dad getting them to the car and home on the double. On the longest car ride home of her life, Kelis doesn't seem to

SO IT DOESN'T HAVE TO BE YOU

understand why if daddy won't hug her or kiss her or tell her he loves her, why he can't at least buy her things. She understands daddy may not be the most emotional man, for she was not a very emotional child, and she didn't like to be hugged or kissed either, but she still FELT love and she knew her mom loved her. When mom remembered that Kelis really wanted something and picked it up for a good report card or good test, she spoke one of Kelis' love languages. It was not so much that the gift was tangible, than that it showed that mom was paying attention to all that was around her and what Kelis desired. Why doesn't daddy understand me, she wondered to herself.

      As they pulled up to the house… Kaila grabbed both bags full of gifts and ran them up to the house without saying one word to dad. She then opened the door and said, "Come on Kelis we're HOME now." Kelis obediently go out the car and rubbed her eyes as Kaila slammed the car door behind her and ran to mom. When she focused she saw

WHY ME?

her mom glaring at her father from the stairs. Kaila told mom everything, thought Kelis. And when she saw mommy smile and call to her, she ran up the lawn to her mom, who picked her up and hugged her. For the first time in about three hours Kelis exhaled and let go. She was back home, in the arms of her mother, the only person who REALLY loved her, and she was… safe.

SO IT DOESN'T HAVE TO BE YOU

Chapter One

If ever there was a more unlikely candidate to win Kelis back over to the side where she wanted a daddy, one would think it was this man her mother married. Randy was a childless, very tall, light skinned man, who Kelis didn't necessarily appreciate coming and stealing her mom's time and love from her. When they met she made it clear she didn't like him, or any other man for that matter, and Randy knew it. Yet, for some strange reason, unexplainable by anyone, he won her over.

He respected Kelis' space and let her come to her own realizations about him. He never forced her to do anything or hang out with him. He just let her exist. And as time went on, they tolerated each other and that turned into a true blue daddy-daughter relationship. Wherever he went, Kelis was sure to follow. Since he couldn't have children, Kelis was the closest thing he had to a

WHY ME?

daughter. You would have never thought this relationship started so rocky.

Eventually Randy married Kelis' mom Gwyneth and along with Chase (Kelis' older brother), and Kaila, they became a family. And the next year, by a miracle, Randy and Gwyneth had a child, whom they named Dionne. If ever there was a cute baby that looked like a china doll, it was Dionne. At first Kelis was worried because now Randy had a daughter of his own, but his love never changed for Kelis. He continued to take them all to the park, Chuck E Cheese, backyard crab fests and everything else that makes family fun.

Then, Randy got sick. They said he had cancer, which Kelis didn't comprehend. She just knew her dad was slowing down and she didn't like it one bit. She wondered if maybe if she prayed really hard then God would hear her and make her dad better. SO she

SO IT DOESN'T HAVE TO BE YOU

prayed, all the time, begging God to make her dad feel better. She had been in church all her 7 years on the Earth, so she figured God would grant a simple request to keep the only dad she'd ever known, the only man in her life who reciprocated her love, alive and well.

1996 had been a rough year for Kelis, first her dad got sick in February, then later that year her goldfish died. She remembered when Randy took her to get the fish, and it hurt her immensely that during the funeral for the fish, her brother and sister laughed at her misfortune. Yet, even in the hospital, Randy called Kelis to express his sorrow for their fish and wanted her to know that he loved her and that everything was going to be ok.

During the time Randy was ill, he was in and out of the hospital. For a short time, near fall, he stayed at home for a while and got worse. So Kelis prayed harder and harder. It seemed the

WHY ME?

harder she prayed, the worse he got. And eventually Randy went back to the hospital. She never knew that the day he went back was the last time she would see him alive.

    Kelis knew God would answer her, because all of her Sunday school teachers and mom had told her that God hears the children and He answers them. So she stayed praying, never giving up. She exhausted herself, even trying to bargain with God, hoping He would just do her ONE favor.

    Well, it never happened. On November 16, 1996, Randy died. At first Kelis couldn't believe what happened. She figured she would ask God one more time to bring her father back to her. SO she begged and pleaded while mommy went to take care of some things.

SO IT DOESN'T HAVE TO BE YOU

When mommy came back with the balloons and cards from the hospital, she brightened slightly, hoping, praying, believing Randy would come through the door, with the smile that always made her feel loved and like she deserved to be loved, like she mattered to someone because they wanted her to matter. With the hugs that let her know she too was special. Yet all she saw was the defeated look on her family's face and the pain in her mother's eyes as she hugged her close.

The next few days were hard on Kelis. Getting ready to give a "home going" to the dad she prayed for. "Why did God do this to me" she thought, walking into the funeral home for the wake. All she could remember was belting out "The Sun will come out tomorrow" and remembering the father who loved her so. Who always listened to her sing, watched her dance, and praised everything she ever did. And for the first time, the words had no

WHY ME?

meaning. God took the sun from her when he took Randy from her family. Everyone was miserable and life just wasn't the same.

At the funeral the next day, she stood there in her white dress. At the family's request, most everyone was dressed in white because Randy would not have wanted anyone to be sad. Kelis reflected on all the good times with Randy: Her graduation from elementary school, Kaila's prom, buying the house they lived in, going to Chuck E Cheese, the many hugs and kisses, trips to everywhere and trips to nowhere, patient evenings spent teaching Kelis new things, nights out to dinner, late nights eating everyone's leftovers.

As she stared down at the dead face of her father, her daddy, the love her own father didn't give her and she no longer wanted was prevalent. The feeling was fury, pain, anger, frustration, hate. Over and over again these

SO IT DOESN'T HAVE TO BE YOU

feelings went until they spiraled into wrath. Kelis began to cry, harder than she'd cried before. Nothing had ever impacted her so badly. Looking over to Kaila, right next to her, was screaming and crying, dealing with her own loss.

      She drifted away and wondered, "Where is God and how could He do this to me?" The pain was unbearable and suddenly Kelis wanted to die too, just to stop the pain. She was absolutely devastated.

      They went back to their home after burying her dad and had repast for the guests. Kelis felt a need to pray. She wanted to pray. She had so much to say to God; so much she felt she deserved to know. She wanted answers so badly. If the crap that people said was true, God wouldn't have ever allowed the only father she ever really had or knew, to leave her life never to return. God couldn't be that cruel and heartless, could He? Yet He did it to Kelis and her

WHY ME?

family. And 10 to 1 He never thought how this would hurt anyone. They say He has a grand design and everything is for a reason, but for what reason would He take a father away from His children? Didn't He understand that Kelis needed Randy around? That her self-esteem was growing and she was finally fully happy?

    As she sat and pondered in the bathroom that Randy designed and tiled all on his own, she decided that God could not possibly be all that people say He is. He could not possibly love his children, if He'd take the physical representation of himself away from her.

    That was the day Kelis decided there was no more God. Not in her life. People could believe the hype if they wanted to, but the pain was too much. November 20, 1996, Kelis' spirit died, her faith died, her desire for God died. And the only one she had any faith, trust, and comfort in, was the only one

SO IT DOESN'T HAVE TO BE YOU

she felt really never left her and had her best interest at heart: MOM.

    And she left the bathroom, leaving God to wherever he wanted to be. And she didn't talk to him again until 2002.

WHY ME?

SO IT DOESN'T HAVE TO BE YOU

Chapter Two

"Smile" the photographer urged. Kelis glared at him. Her best friend, Chari, looked at her and said "Come ONNN, we're graduating high school, your GPA is INSANE, you're going to the school YOU chose, and your hair looks fabulous!" Kelis grinned at the mere THOUGHT of getting up out of Mason High School, from under all the pressure of being the only 16 year old in the graduating class, always trying to do better, and knowing that they didn't see her potential because of her quiet demeanor, and as quiet as it's kept, the color of her skin. Silent thoughts of NCAT, the school she chose, historically black, crept into her mind. She was giving the photographer the smiles he begged for as she thought of the history… the A&T Four, civil right activists and all, the prestige of the Blue and Gold, and the unbelievable AGGIE PRIDE. She was proud to be going there in August and to finally wear the blue and gold she adored as a child.

WHY ME?

As she finished up her photographs, the photographer said "You're a natural kid, don't ever forget it. Best of luck in college." Kelis smiled and thanked the man for his generosity and ran out with her best friend.

"Can you BELIEVE the four years are UP?!?!!" she shrieked. Chari looked at her and laughed, "Yes I can believe it! We worked, well… YOU worked hard for this… we deserve to be getting out of here. Four years of hell! I will miss this place though. To think, when we're rich and famous, good old Mason High will be oh so important…" Kelis responded, "Hell, maybe then we can get our own auditorium. All this time, we raise money and the school looks worse every year. Maybe they will restore it to its former glory?"

SO IT DOESN'T HAVE TO BE YOU

They get stopped in the hall by Khalil, an underclassman, but a sweetheart still. He hugs Kelis and starts talking "Look at you, all dressed up looking fly. Slick, you never cease to amaze me..." Kelis grins at him and does the "diva spin" while responding "Ohhh stop...no, GO ON!" And they all laugh.

Khalil was an underclassmen but he was still older than Kelis by a year. Kelis was always exceptionally gifted, so she started first grade at four years old. If her birthday had been a tad earlier in the year, she'd have graduated at fifteen. But there was already a large distinction between her and her graduating class. Even though she usually liked older men, there was something about Khalil that sparked her interest. They had been cool since she was in the tenth grade, and she considered him cool people, so being seen with him wasn't exactly a bad thing. After all, the class of 2004 had crowned her moodiest. If they really tallied she would have beat her male

WHY ME?

superlative winner by a landslide. The problem wasn't so much that Kelis was MEAN, it just was that she didn't allow too much to go on in her presence. She was 100 at all times, and as quiet as it was kept, Khalil liked her, just as much as she liked him. They were just both too stupid to see what would happen. Fear of it working was Kelis' problem. She had never exactly been in a place to be 100% happy.

    So, as she and Khalil are all hugged up in the hallway, Chari is looking at them wondering WHY they won't get themselves together. "Alright Khalil, lemme go get out these clothes. I can't walk around Mason looking all royal, I might get hung." Kelis gave him another hug, which he took full advantage of, and a peck on the cheek and walked away. "Or beheaded" Khalil called. Kelis laughed as Chari responded, "If she gets beheaded, I'm castrating YOU." They all laughed again as Kelis and Chari went into the bathroom to change their clothes.

SO IT DOESN'T HAVE TO BE YOU

In the stalls away from ears and eyes, Kelis starts up. "Chari, he's gorgeous, and those eyes are like liquid. They just pierce right through you!" No response. They keep getting dressed. Chari finally says "Well you both act like you don't see the sparks. I think he's cute too, but I KNOW you guys could work. He's mellow and you're red hot. He's warm and inviting, you're ice cold."

Chari comes out the stall in her usual attire, much different from the floral print she had on for her pictures. Her grunge look fit her personality but not how she looked to the eye. She had on her black jeans with the zippers and a long sleeved black t-shirt, with some rock legend on it, which she had made herself. She had torn it to make it a little more edgy and placed fishnet underneath the rips and had on some black boots. She took her hair down and observed Kelis' outfit.

WHY ME?

Kelis had a style all her own, and generally wore what she wanted to wear. Today was a "cute day" light blue fitted jeans, with a chocolate brown cami and an eggshell sweater, complete with chocolate brown ankle boots.

"Cute", they both said to each other and laughed. To the mirror they went, with Chari pulling her makeup out her pockets and Kelis looking in her purse for her makeup bag. They completed their looks with the appropriate eyeliners and glosses. Kelis blew herself a kiss in the mirror and smiled. When she looked like this, she could see her beauty, but there were some days where it just was NOT coming together. Thank God today was not one of those days. She knew she'd see Khalil later and she loved the attention he gave her, like nobody else was in the hallway.

Chari on the other hand, was in the mirror practicing the mean mugs

SO IT DOESN'T HAVE TO BE YOU

Kelis had taught her. Each girl possessed the personality the other had and NEEDED for the looks they portrayed, so they just taught each other. Kelis was learning this sweet pea smile thing, and Chari was trying hard to give people faces and not words. It went alright, and they always were there for each other.

Kelis moved to Oceanfront when she was 6, 3rd grade… and Chari had lived there basically her whole life. Upon entering the evil Mrs. Stayle's class, Kelis happened upon Chari and from then they were the BEST of friends. Right before middle school they fell out and it only made them stronger in the end. Anything that ever happened, they ran to each other and it was there they found solace. When everything was turbulent, they could call each other and it would be okay. Advice was exchanged; secrets, dreams, and fears were shared; life was an oyster that they chose to tackle together. Kelis knew she was blessed to have Chari around because nobody else understood her,

WHY ME?

and Chari looked beyond what Kelis SAID, into her heart and understood what she THOUGHT.

    The girls left the bathroom and decided to get some lunch. As they walked they met up with Cheyenne, a sweet, yet brilliant girl from the Philippines. She was a welcomed addition to the group, since she never could FIT anywhere, and in a way, neither could Kelis and Chari. So together, they, and anyone else they saw fit, were untouchable, insomuch that people can't handle what they don't understand. Kelis didn't need to be understood by others, because she understood she was who she was without them.

    At the bodega they ordered sandwiches and got drinks and candy and whatever else, and chit chatted about leaving Mason, which Cheyenne had only been at for a year. Chari

SO IT DOESN'T HAVE TO BE YOU

started up. "So Kelis what's up with prom"?

Kelis smiles at her and responds, "Well I wish you were going, but that's another story. I spoke to Gad the other day and he's psyched about it. My dress fitting is later today, for the first part, to make sure I like it and everything. I have no idea what I'm going to do without Kaila here. She's going to be in California for something for her job. I am so sad she's not going to be here, but I guess it's meant to be… I am totally ready though. I know it's almost three months away but there's something keeping me SO buzzed about it. Sometimes I wonder if Khalil would have gone with me had I asked him. I never thought to though…"

"Humph" Cheyenne interjects. "You know good and well he'd have jumped at the chance to go with you. I know you said you asked Gad a LONG time ago, but STILL… At least you see

WHY ME?

and talk to Khalil regularly and you guys are somewhat comfortable around each other. I STILL think you should see what Khalil says. Gad won't mind. It's not HIS prom…"

"Oh what the hell EVERRRR" Chari says, while they walk out the store. "You know Gad's NOT going to be happy. He's told his whole family that he's taking you, and it's too soon to change all that. Now, if he acts up, I say you cut him loose and get Khalil, but as for right now, it looks dumb. You asked him to take you, now you're ready to drop him for the hazel eyes that make you melt? Come on, this is SO not like you. And Cheyenne, you ought to be ashamed of yourself."

Chari had always been the voice of reason, but this new edge on her was making her SO real. Both Kelis and Cheyenne loved it. As they walked back to the school they began to talk about the latest buzz. Chari and her boyfriend

SO IT DOESN'T HAVE TO BE YOU

of almost a year, Jasyn, had finally decided to do the do. Kelis was a known virgin, and was cool with it. Cheyenne on the other hand was so mysterious and ambiguous in her speech you'd never really know. So as far as everyone else is concerned, Chari is the first one to "go".

"How is Jasyn?" Cheyenne inquires. Chari looks at the floor and back up into Kelis' eyes. Kelis responds on cue "Cheyenne, she's regretting it, because she's moving and Jasyn is not. Also with college so soon she wonders how long they can even stay together. She's also regretting dating so late in the game. Even though Jasyn is great and she loves him, they don't connect on enough levels for her to say she'd want to stay with him forever."

"Damn" Cheyenne says, while letting out a sigh. "That's friendship for you. One look and you can say

WHY ME?

everything she needs said. Kelis makes a face that says, "It is what it is".

And then as if on a timer for all things juicy, the bell rings. Cheyenne says, "Listen, I've got a class, but I'll get with you two later!" They both say goodbye to her and begin to walk over to some lunch tables outside. This final year they had the same lunch and free period afterwards. Then, while Chari had some photography courses, Kelis went on home. But today, she was staying for the newspaper and to maybe see Khalil, who was an avid hall roamer and liked to just chill.

As they sit down Chari says "So, tell me about the dress." Kelis' eyes light up as she begins to explain the royal ivory and gold dress she designed herself. Chari smiles because as much as Kelis loves a lot of things, clothes and shoes have always taken the cake. Besides, this was her best friend, why shouldn't she be happy?

SO IT DOESN'T HAVE TO BE YOU

Deep down Chari sort of wanted to go to prom. Jasyn wasn't exactly the most outgoing of persons, and Chari wasn't going to force him. So they were just going to go to a show and dinner or something. And THAT Kelis wasn't happy with. It wasn't even satisfactory for the wonderful night she was going to have.

The best part of Kelis and Chari's relationship was that they could do things at the same time and consider it bonding. For example, after lunch they had basically a whole period to hang with each other. They leaned back in the chairs and turned on their mp3 players, each loaded with completely different music. Kelis wrote and Chari drew. And about thirty minutes later, they compared what they did in complete silence. Yet, it was bonding. Kelis would take a bullet for Chari and Chari would so the same for Kelis. They were no longer friends, they were sisters. An eternal bond that could never be broken.

WHY ME?

They hugged and parted ways after the free period. Chari to the photography room, and Kelis to the English room, to see Dr. D'Alessi about the newspaper, and to just mess around before the end of classes.

He handed her a camera and said, "I know you're not a photographer, but I need some pictures for this edition of the paper. So, I wrote down some classes you can go to for the next two periods and capture some Mason Rams in action. Please make it really diverse and have fun with it. You can even BE in the pictures if you want. Have a ball!"

Dr. D'Alessi was by far one of Kelis' favorite teachers, right next to Mr. Count, the business teacher she adored, Ms. Lavita, the English teacher that inspired her, and Mr. Dafino, the Economics and Government teacher that always kept her in stitches. In four

SO IT DOESN'T HAVE TO BE YOU

years, these were the only teachers she had really formed a relationship with. Dr. D' Alessi knew that, and he also knew how pliable Kelis was for him and the paper. Very few people could just GIVE Kelis a task.

Dr. D' Alessi took full advantage of that and Kelis was on her way.

The first place she stopped was Mr. Count's Business class. Khalil was in that class and she was not about to just pass up his class. She knocked and walked right in.

Mr. Count said, "There she is. I was expecting you!" He spoke to his class while making gestures at her. "If you want to know whose grades it is you're competing with, it's hers. She's taken EVERY business class, with me I might add, and never ended under a 97. For most of you, that's a dream, for her, well, she was pissed because she wanted 100."

WHY ME?

Kelis looked at him with a twinkle in her eye and said "Listen, I'm not here to intimidate people. I'm here to take pictures. So just do what you were doing and I'll be in the corner doing what I do."

She took the seat cat a corner to Khalil and crossed her legs. Mr. Count began to talk about law. Business law was the first class she took of his, so she remembered everything and was enthralled. As he wrote some insurance equations on the board she snapped a photo.

Whenever someone said something completely stupid or wrong, she'd look at Khalil and make a remark. He'd crack up laughing at her. She had Accounting with Khalil the year prior so Mr. Count was used to their antics in his classroom. He shook his head at them and laughed.

SO IT DOESN'T HAVE TO BE YOU

Kelis stood up and began to walk around the class taking random pictures of students not paying attention and the like. Before she knew it, Mr. Count had her up there, being bombarded with questions about Business law, and mainly how to pass the final. She was sharing with them and taking pictures at the same time.

About 10 minutes before the bell rang, she looked at her cell phone and said "Oh no, I've been in here with you guys about a half hour. I've gotta go take more pictures! It's been real, thanks for letting me bother you guys." She waved at Mr. Count and began to leave. Khalil said, "Slick, I'll see you later ma." She turned around and winked and blew him a kiss and switched out the classroom. She heard the catcalling and cajoling as she closed the door.

WHY ME?

She flew up the stairs to the Photography room where she had Chari stand in front of her and take a picture of her taking a picture of her. How artsy Chari thought. Kelis quickly ran the scenario down in the Business room and Chari said "Y'all can't keep your hands off each other; neither can you remember you're in school. Y'all not the only ones in here!" Kelis laughed and said 'I gotta go; I'll see you after school"

Kelis went around to some more classes and took pictures. Of course she had to find Khalil and get one with him. It turned out really good, so she was going to convince Mr. Dafino to make it a color photo in the yearbook.

The 9th period bell rang and Kelis went to her locker. As she was humming Ying Yang twins, she started rocking her

SO IT DOESN'T HAVE TO BE YOU

hips dancing to her own humming. Khalil came up behind her and grabbed her waist tightly as he hugged her. Kelis turned her head to make sure it was Khalil. It felt like him and smelled like him, but at Mason, guys think a big butt is for whoever has enough guts to approach the owner.

She let out a sigh of relief when she saw it really WAS him. She hugged him back and said, "What's up sweetie? You ready for the end of the year? Next year you're out of here!" He smiled at her and said, "I guess. I'm alright Slick, I just came to check you out and see what you were doing. You smell good by the way."

She shook her head at him. "Thanks I guess. I try and smell good all the time." She laughs. "I'm going to the newspaper meeting to see what the paper will look like for next week and to give him the pictures I took today. Pick some for the paper, and try and get

WHY ME?

Dafino to put some in the Yearbook. Why do you ask? You were coming with me?"

Khalil looked at her. She stared back. "I guess that means no." She slammed her locker shut and hugged him. "I'll see you later babes". She switched away from him.

She walked the three flights to the English room and slung her bag on the desk. "Chari" she pouted, while still in the doorway, "He gonna ask me a million questions about what I'm doing and where I am going and then has the nerve to not even come with me or acknowledge that I said I was coming here."

Chari's eyes get larger as if she's trying to say something and Kelis ignores her.

SO IT DOESN'T HAVE TO BE YOU

"And" she continues, "He said he'd see me later like it was all important and he didn't even-"

Kelis is cut off by the familiar arms holding her from behind. As much as she wants to turn around and two piece him in the chest, she can't. He's always had that effect on her. She gives Chari the death stare because she KNOWS Chari saw him and never responded. She liked putting Kelis in compromising situations.

"You really mad at me?" he whispers in her ear still holding her. Kelis just pouts. He whispers again "I think you're not mad anymore, you just like when I hold you like this" and he tightens his grip on her. She sighs and turns around to look at him. "I'm gonna slap you Khalil. Why do you ask me all this stuff and then act like it doesn't matter? Who feels like being bothered?"

WHY ME?

Dr. D'Alessi says, "I hate to break up this lover's spat but I need you to upload these pictures from this camera, and go to the dark room and develop these." He hands her two rolls of film and a digital camera.

In the darkroom, Kelis usually spent her time developing the master plan for her life. School, work, marriage, children, friendships, all clouded her mind as she also developed the photographs. Mason High had not given her all the joy she had hoped, but she'd completed what she was there to do.

Today, however, was one of those days. The days when Khalil followed her to the darkroom. She liked having him around, but at the same time, she got no real peace and quiet at home, so he was imposing himself into her "me time". As she dipped and swirled, processing the negatives quietly, she began to hum different songs that she knew. She was

SO IT DOESN'T HAVE TO BE YOU

happy to be able to just…be. And then, as if on cue, Khalil breaks the silence.

"You ever wonder what is gonna happen when we get out of here? How much will change?" he asked.

"Yeah. Every time I get a chance." she responded. "Even though you still have one more year of absolute hell in front of you. Though it can't be that bad, you've always had football and track to occupy you. "

    Khalil had been the best Safety Mason High had in years, and he was proud of it. Kelis had rarely missed a home game, stopping by between her busy schedule at school, home, and church; though she wondered if he ever noticed. Probably not.

WHY ME?

      That was always the problem. She did so much, and nobody ever noticed. Neither did they care. Yet it was better than not knowing what was going on. If you knew what to expect out of life, you were more able to cope with it. A very skewed philosophy for a sixteen year old to have, but not every sixteen year old had Kelis' life.

As she continues to reflect on her life, her own personal hardships and the battle within herself…

Another interruption by Khalil.

"Football is great, but sometimes I wonder is it really what I want to do in life. You spend your whole life training to be great, but there's always someone greater. You get older and try to stay on top, but there's always gonna be someone younger, faster, smarter, more agile, more flexible, more of whatever

SO IT DOESN'T HAVE TO BE YOU

you don't have. Every time I walk onto a football field, I pray to God my ACL doesn't tear. How many athletes had a career that was over before it started because of a torn ACL, or a bone broken in just the wrong spot, or they find out they have some unfixable problem and they can never play anything again?"

He sighs.

"I just want to live my life Kelis. I want to be happy and not worry about these things, I have enough that can make or break me. I want my mom to be proud and not worried. I want to be a legend, but not at the cost of going wherever the wind takes me."

She smiles at him. "Well, the great and terrible thing about life is that to try and enjoy it, you have to relinquish control."

Being a complete control freak herself, Kelis knew what she was

WHY ME?

saying; and also knew that if someone told her that she'd have to tell them to stick it where the sun doesn't shine, but K was different, he listened to her. His laid back attitude allowed for adjustments to his life.

He gave her a knowing smile. A smile that soothed her in accounting class. The very same smile that she loved in 10th grade, gym class. She would never forget it. Though she knew Khalil would forget her... after all, she was leaving, going her separate way from him. She opened her mouth to finally spill all of how she felt.

"Khalil, you are such a sweetheart. You always made me smile. And I never said anything but I really-"

A voice came from the distance "Kelis, I need five dollars."

SO IT DOESN'T HAVE TO BE YOU

Say what?, Kelis thought to herself. Only one other person could possibly know where she was.

"Domenick." she responded. And he laughed. Hysterically.

Kelis was so mad she could cry. Domenick had a knack for always ruining something, especially when it came to Khalil. They were cool, but, this was just too much.

She reached in her bag and handed him five dollars through the darkroom door. Waving her hand, a symbol for "go away" he started with questions.

"Who's in there?"

"No one. Just me."

WHY ME?

"I heard more than one voice"

"I'm playing the radio." She knew he'd make himself comfortable if he knew Khalil was there.

"I didn't hear any music."

"It was a commercial D. Leave me alone. I'm working."

"Is Khalil in there?"

"No! Please…"

"Alright, alright. If you see him, let him know we're about to get some football goin'."

Kelis sighed. "Alright D."

She heard him go running down the hallway, and she knew Khalil would leave not too long after. He always did. And she was never upset. He loved football, and she was just a friend… a quiet one at that. He had plenty of females jockin' him. He had no need for her anyway.

SO IT DOESN'T HAVE TO BE YOU

She said to him "I know you heard him. They're going to play."

"I know that Kelis. I heard him." he responded, "But, how many more times will I be able to just sit here and talk with you? Football will be there when we're done. And they'll let me play. They always do."

She smiles at him, and quickly remembering what she was going to say, goes completely left field in conversation.

"So where are you going to apply?" she asks him.

"Not too sure. I'm narrowing it down still."

WHY ME?

"You know, you don't have much time honey…"

"Yes, I know. I'll have it done soon enough, you know senior year makes or breaks scholarships for football player-"

"Oh, that's right!" she interjects, "I forgot all about that! I'm sure it'll all be alright though"

      As if on cue, her phone starts to ring. Crime Mob's "Knuck If You Buck" invades her private time.

"State your name and your purpose." she commands the private caller.

She listens closely and then hangs up the phone, turning it off as she closes it.

      Khalil is in his same spot, on the darkroom couch, looking at her with those light brown eyes, glittering in the dim of the darkroom. She says to him:

SO IT DOESN'T HAVE TO BE YOU

"People like to call me for no reason at all. Just, none."

She sighs. "I'm finished."

He waves her to the couch with his hand and they sit together. And they just talk. Her head is on his shoulder, and his arm is wrapped around her. And they do nothing but talk. She opens some of her fears to him, some of her desires, and what she wants to achieve out of her life. And he understands her, and he listens, and he doesn't try anything funny. They merely exist in those moments, and Kelis wonders where this friend was all of her life.

WHY ME?

SO IT DOESN'T HAVE TO BE YOU

Chapter 3

Graduation was quickly approaching and Kelis wasn't exactly certain she was ready to leave Mason, and more importantly, her family. The time had come where she had to grow up, and for a 16 year old, that was way too soon and too fast. She had swelling doubts and decided to see if she could find some people also fearing leaving their family and going to the illustrious NCAT in the summer's end.

    Her keyboard clicked away in her bedroom as she searched. And there it was. Www.hbcu-connect.com. In the cafe she saw plenty of people, not only going to school, but already at historically black colleges and universities. SO as she created her profile, she started talking to old and future Aggies alike, developing a sincere relationship with a few people.

WHY ME?

One of the site administrators, trusted by the creator of the website, was, in fact an Aggie. He spoke to Kelis on a daily basis, informing her of things she needed to know. They developed a cool relationship and Kelis felt comfortable talking to him. He was calming her fears. Yes. Cooper was exactly who she needed to soothe her fears.

On the journey in getting to know more about NCAT, Cooper linked her to his exclusive Aggie website, Xclusively Aggie, where she ended up befriending many, including a first year like herself, Kacey, and some upperclassmen, Rodney, Deon, and Christina. Time was winding down and Kelis found all her fears soothed. Yet she also found herself in another conundrum.

Talking to Cooper all the time had made her like him. He was almost 21 and it had never dawned on Kelis that he was still at NCAT with no degree. All

SO IT DOESN'T HAVE TO BE YOU

she knew is he was nice, and thought she was pretty and always made her feel good about herself.

In the months to come, she'd learn more about him and herself than she ever knew before.

On Prom day, Kelis spent a great deal of time with her mother. They talked about Kelis growing up, and she really wanted to cry. It was like she was leaving that day for college, rather than just going to prom. She also found out that day, that the family dog was missing. She wasn't very worried because Buddah liked to run around the neighborhood and always came home. What didn't make much sense was that they said she'd been missing for a long time.

In her mother's dress shoppe; she tried on her dress once more. Still too big in the waist, they contemplated whether or not to make more changes.

WHY ME?

"Still too big there!" said the tailor, in a thick African accent. He was shaking his head, because this was the only prom dress coming out of the shop for Mason High School. Unlike the previous years, Kelis' mom had shut the place down for her silk embroidered dress with the precious rhinestones she adored so much.

As Kelis took the dress off, she said to her mother "Just leave it, it's not a big deal." And off she went to get her nails finished. On her nails she had the very same diamond embroidery that was on the hood, tail, and top of her dress, complete with small rhinestones in the center.

At Mason, prom was a big deal. Before you went to the first party location, you came to the school to show off your transformation, and if you were lucky, your date. Complete with hair, nails, makeup, dress, shoes, and Gad in tow, Kelis headed to the school

SO IT DOESN'T HAVE TO BE YOU

with her friends to make her red carpet debut.

On the way to the school, she was scared to death. She thought she was going to fall right out of that limo and crack her head on the pavement.

She looked seriously at Gad and said "Listen, you have to make sure I don't fall. I feel crazy."

He nodded.

She said it again.

He nodded, and this time said "I heard you. I'm not going to let you fall."

They arrived at the school and she placed the hood on her head. This hood was her super dramatic mother and Kaila's creation.

Gad helped her out of the limo, because she certainly couldn't see, and she walked to the red carpet.

WHY ME?

Questions of who it could be flooded the crowd, and when she stepped on the carpet, she took the hood off and the crowd cheered. Nobody knew she was really going, and it didn't help that her date was, gorgeous to say the very least about Gad's appearance.

She felt good going down the aisle in her dress, winking at Chari along the way, who decided prom was not for her.

As she got to the end of the runway, she saw her sister's boyfriend Bobby there. Kelis reflected on the fact that Kaila wasn't there. She was away in California on business and had assigned Bobby to the special task of making sure there were enough pictures for her to feel like she was there.

SO IT DOESN'T HAVE TO BE YOU

And Bobby was there, taking pictures like the paparazzi, and he had brought money for Kelis. He always brought her money. Secret was, Bobby had loved Kaila since the day he met her, and so he knew Kelis was the best way to get her, so he took advantage of Kaila's love for Kelis and Dionne, and always brought presents.

Dionne was at the end of the runway too, clapping and screaming, as usual. Dionne was too funny, going "That's MY sister" and laughing. It seems Kelis' whole family had showed up for the event, and in that instant she missed Kaila, and wished more than anything that she was there with her.

Overall prom was a pretty awesome night. Her date was sweet and respectful, and was a total gentleman. He did seem a little stiff though. Kelis knew it had to be because

WHY ME?

they had actually met in church and he didn't know how "regular" she was. It was cool though, par for the course. She would have rather been with him than anyone else, except maybe Khalil. She knew that would have been awesome to do.

And as quiet as it was kept, sometimes she wanted to actually take Khalil with her. It was easy to be herself around him, and everyone wants that.

She arrived home around 6 a.m. The next morning, and sat in her mother's room, in her stepdad's big comfy chair and told the whole night's story.

She went to sleep with happy thoughts and peaceful dreams, as she slept.

SO IT DOESN'T HAVE TO BE YOU

As a whirlwind, graduation snuck right up after prom.

Kelis was so ready. She stood in the gym with Chari and they couldn't seem to get their composure. They didn't speak, just smiled and stared. There were no words to express the joy of completing something you'd worked so hard for.

Yet at the same time, this is the place where you grew up, where you started to find yourself. And you're leaving the people that helped mold and shape you.

For Kelis, the only real things she'd miss about Mason were her favorite teachers, and being able to see and interact with Khalil and Chari on a daily. Everything else was just extras.

WHY ME?

In the auditorium pomp and circumstance started to play. As Kelis walked in, her family abandoned all the rules that state that you're supposed to be quiet.

Kelis had not invited her father, but her mom, her stepdad Kenny (mom married him in '99), both her sisters, her brother, and her niece and nephews were there. And they made so much noise for her that you would have sworn she had won the Presidency.

Kelis felt so accomplished. She had not earned the spot of Valedictorian or Salutatory, but she did graduate high school with high honors at a fresh 16, and that mattered to her more than anything. Kelis had never been one to like education much, but she had a knack for it.

SO IT DOESN'T HAVE TO BE YOU

And she did it. They called her name and she graduated. She walked proudly across the stage as her family went berserk and her sister ran across the front of the auditorium to give her blue and gold (Aggie Colors) gifts and scream "Aggie Pride". She never felt as accomplished as she placed her tassel from one side to the other.

In the gym, they had cake and punch to celebrate and she took pictures with mom and Kaila. Dionne was mad because Kelis never took pictures with her. Spoiled was Dionne's middle name, not realizing they were forcing Kelis to take the few pictures she did

All her life she had been beyond brilliant, and she reflected on her mother proudly standing by in family discussions, talking about how brilliant and wonderful Kelis was. And never once did Kelis think that in time to come,

WHY ME?

she'd fail her mother in more ways than she'd be able to imagine.

SO IT DOESN'T HAVE TO BE YOU

Chapter 4

Kaila, Kelis, Dionne, and their mom Gwyneth and stepdad Kenny went down to NCAT on August 9, 2004. They were dropping Kelis off for Orientation. You could tell Gwyneth was not happy about leaving her baby in North Carolina on her solo. And as happy as she tried to be, Kelis could discern a look of uncertainty on her mother's face, especially when they met her roommate Carrie.

Carrie had that room looking like hell had frozen over. Gwyneth was like "This is a mess. This looks crazy. I don't think I like this". As Carrie apologized and explained why the room looked like that, Gwyneth just walked out. And the family followed.

WHY ME?

They went shopping for different things to go in Kelis' room and helped her get it all set up. Kaila was so proud of her sister and let everyone know it.

At the last dinner together before they left, they only spoke of happy times. They went back to Kelis' room one more time, and Gwyneth prayed. After praying, she gave her daughter more money and kissed her. Kelis waved as they drove away. Then she went up to her room and cried.

It was the first time she had been this far from her family, and it was hard for her to realize she was alone. And alone was not good for her.

Carrie came back to the room and saw her crying. She tried to console her new roommate, but she was no help. Carrie was crying herself and lived thirty minutes away!

SO IT DOESN'T HAVE TO BE YOU

Help was coming though. She met up with Kacey, and they became better friends quickly. They kept each other strong. Kacey's roommate Star was awesome as well, a quiet girl, but very funny and insightful. Then you had Jameela, who was loud and raunchy and kept everyone in stitches. They were all friends and that friendship kept things tight. The tension was leaving.

Kelis was in her room talking to her friend Shak on the phone. He had become her friend over the summer and was always around for her. They were just talking about how much Kelis missed home, and he was trying to keep her strong so she could do what she needed to.

She was telling him about the pep rallies, the Greeks on campus, and the fun she was having. She also told him about the outrageous price of textbooks and how much fun orientation was. A weeklong celebration of entering

WHY ME?

college and it was getting better by the day.

Then the phone beeped, informing her of another call. She asked him to hold on, and clicked over. It was Kacey, who they called KP.

"Yeah?" she said.

"Kelis come downstairs", KP demanded.

"Why?"

"Someone wants to meet you".

"Well I'm settled in for the night, so tell them to come back tomorrow" Kelis stated.

"Kelis, it's 7:30" Kacey said in a tired voice.

SO IT DOESN'T HAVE TO BE YOU

"I don't want to meet anyone, I'm on the phone." and with that they hung up the phone.

She went back to talking to Shak, who was laughing at her clear dislike for being interrupted while talking to him. And the line beeped again. She answered.

"Room 211 A state your name and your purpose."

"You know, you're gonna make me leave" said a male voice.

"Uh, who is this?"

"Cooper."

WHY ME?

Kelis almost dropped the phone on the floor. She definitely did not want to see him, talk to him, and be around him. For her Cooper was spelled T-R-O-U-B-L-E and she wanted no parts of him, literally or figuratively.

"Well, I'm in the room already."

He bargained with her to just come down and say hi, and so she did. This was her first mistake.

She told Shak she would hit him up online after she met this guy and he wished her luck.

She went downstairs and walked past this group of thug wannabe's to KP and said:

SO IT DOESN'T HAVE TO BE YOU

"Alright, where is he?"

She snickered and pointed at the largest in the group. Kelis was horrified and prayed it didn't show up on her face. This fool had the audacity to come up to the school looking like a Thriller reject. Hair all over his face, clothes straight scruffy, he looked like he crawled out of a pile of hot garbage. Kelis was glad he didn't smell like it.

She smiled and extended her hand, and he pulled her in for a hug. She looked over at KP and rolled her eyes. She stared at him.

"Ok, I met you, is this over?"

Cooper smiled at her. He had a nice smile. "Well, it's whatever."

WHY ME?

They all chatted for a little while, and then KP decided it was time to get ready to go out for the night.

Kelis smiled and walked away. Before entering back into her building she stated "Nice to meet you." and let the door close behind her.

A couple weeks later they went to the "Gorilla Thrilla" at Club Allusions, held by the sexy, smart, and classy men of Alpha Phi Alpha fraternity incorporated.

There was this guy there, who decided he would drink before he got there and snatched Kelis up. She was looking around for someone to get her out of the hands of this madman, and an associate Haley, stepped in and grabbed her, while yelling at the guy and slapping him around. They were quite

SO IT DOESN'T HAVE TO BE YOU

protective of Kelis since she was a 16 year old among a crowd of 18 and older.

She went and sat in the corner, indicating that she was on the next thing smokin' out of that club. Her friends stayed near her, as nobody was having fun. Until the Alphas showed up.

Those men came in and shut the place down. Dancing and stepping, the place got lively. And then, the same fool that was all on Kelis, had picked this one girl up, and slipped and dropped her on the floor.

Kelis had gotten into blogging on www.xanga.com and went right home and wrote.

OK, so I went to a party...Friday after the Gym Jam (bust) for the Alphas...we were originally gonna go to

WHY ME?

the Omega party but u know how it goes down when you do not have your car...so yes we ended up at Allusions. We got there and everything was str8....it was all flava, me and my homies were chillin in the girl circle, dancing, joking, loosening up. And then my trauma for this week:

    This guy comes up behind me and starts dancing or whatever and I'm like okay lets see if we can slow him down, cuz he was moving way too fast for me and the song that was playing (I ain't neva scared).

    So homeboy is shaking like he's got the Holy Ghost and I am like: can a sista get some clarification here? So I'm still tryna work with him, then he starts all tryna pull off all my clothes or w/e and now I am TOO PISSED. I'm tryna get away from this crazy fool and he is FOLLOWING ME... talk about stalkers....then he's like on some "c'mon show me wat u workin with". Little does

SO IT DOESN'T HAVE TO BE YOU

he know that if I woulda had an inch of space he woulda had to work with my foot up his... exactly.

And so here I am fighting a losing ass battle because homie is tryna rip off everything from the shirt down to the panties, and I am sure if he woulda had me alone he woulda tried something funny...

So finally, a new friend I have met, Haley, sees my look of absolute terror and grabs me from him like "what in the hell is going on?"....THANK THE LORD!!!! Because that was the ONLY way I was gonna get away from him...all else had already failed....So naturally I was pissed off. I let my Aggie fam know what was going on, and for the most part they did not know what to say (except for 1 person: LOVE YA!)

I had banned myself from every social function ever created and vowed to not go anywhere else again.....and this morning it finally came to me that I cannot let any little thing that happens to me, stop my progression.

WHY ME?

After hearing her story Cooper tried to convince her not to go any more places. She had been at his apartment to watch a movie and he tried to put the moves on her. He kissed her, and she backed away. She didn't want to explore anything with him; she explained that she just wanted to be friends. He seemed to understand.

Now, all the people she met from Xclusively Aggie had told her not to mess with him, and she had serious intent on following their advice. She trusted Deon and Christine with her life. They were quite the cute little couple, and had no reason to lie to her.

After having bombarded into her room that day, she knew she had made friends for life. They were absolutely awesome, Deon, a military brat, and Christine, a native of the tri- state area, always had Kelis best interest at heart.

SO IT DOESN'T HAVE TO BE YOU

One day, Deon ran the play by play to her and said:

"Kelis, he has issues. He is nowhere near done with school, there's not one, but two girls running around here claiming to be pregnant with his baby. He's sloppy and messy, and you don't need to be involved with him. I promise you he's useless to what you're trying to do. Be friends, just don't get involved."

    Deon was like a brother to Kelis. He looked out for her and kept her focused. She told him she'd be careful and wouldn't get involved with the freak show.

    Later that day, Cooper called Kelis and invited her over. She gave him a simple "no thanks" and he asked why.

"I thought we were having fun" he said.

    She immediately asked him about the pregnant women, the relationship, why he was still in school, and when he didn't answer quickly enough, she hung up on him.

WHY ME?

He came up to the school and invited her over as just friends. She agreed and they watched TV. During the television watching, his mother called and spoke to her, affirming that there were no pregnant women and that her son was a good man. She also told Kelis she was excited to meet her.

His mother seemed nice enough, but Kelis wondered why she needed to affirm her son. She also wondered how she knew Cooper's personal business that way. Still leery of him, Kelis decided to keep her distance.

They hung out more and more over time, and Kelis learned to like him. She also believed every word that came out of his mouth. He told her what she wanted to hear and made it sound twice as sweet. She truly believed he cared about her. Of course she had things she hated about him, but she was willing to overlook those things, after all, she had someone to finally care for her, and love

SO IT DOESN'T HAVE TO BE YOU

her without having to do anything special.

She disliked him most when he talked about sex. He wasn't pressuring her, but he was surely dropping hints. And every time she told him "I don't want to. I don't know you like that. Let it go. I thought you said you'd wait?" And he'd leave it be, to bring it up another day and denied once more.

WHY ME?

SO IT DOESN'T HAVE TO BE YOU

Chapter 5

Homecoming weekend was absolutely awesome. And by awesome, it included all sorts of people Kelis had never seen, and some she hadn't been able to hang out with in a while, because she and Cooper had become connected to the point where they were rarely without each other. Stupidly, Kelis listened to him more than anyone else, and had decided there were not pregnant women, there was no recent breakup, and he really cared for her. Another mistake.

Homecoming brought out the very best in Kelis. The real reason she became an Aggie began to shine through with the various tasks she undertook during homecoming. Making signs, designing floats, having meetings, this was her element, and had she not been so heavily involved with Cooper, she would have been able to do much more.

WHY ME?

Cooper had begun to do more bad than good in Kelis' life. She spent more and more time with him, and less time growing up the regular way. Having fun with her friends wasn't a priority, and hardly an option, as Cooper acted like he was five every time she wanted to do something.

She reflected on the thought of not dealing with him anymore. He seemed to be all talk and no walk, no action ever followed the words he spoke to her, and it was aggravating dealing with him. There was one girl, Roxy that claimed to be pregnant with his child. The girl was miserable. She used to come to his house and leave notes on the door, drive over there unexpectedly and look unbelievably unhappy to see Kelis there. Cooper always reassured her that it was all a lie. And she believed him, as always.

She also considered that one of Cooper's best friends let her know that she was intimate with him, while he was supposed to be getting to know her. He convinced her that because they weren't

SO IT DOESN'T HAVE TO BE YOU

exclusive, it was okay for him to do her how he did. And a very stupid, naïve, trusting 16, she believed him. She felt she had no bearings because after all, they were just "kickin it". Not realizing she deserved respect, and someone to think enough of her to restrain himself. He had done what he set out to do, isolate her, and make her feel like there was nobody but him.

Homecoming ended with a bang, and it also ended with Gwyneth looking for her daughter to be around. She had sent the authorities to her dorm to find her, and was so worried because she had forgotten.

Early Monday morning Kelis heard the phone ring.

"Hello?" she asked groggily, as she wasn't excited to answer the phone.

"KELIS!" her mother screamed.

"Yes?"

"Where have you been, I was so worried. I don't understand. "Gwyneth

WHY ME?

was crying and Kelis almost busted out laughing.

"Homecoming weekend ma" she responded with a sigh.

"Oh! I forgot" Gwyneth said with a chuckle, elated that her child wasn't tucked in some bushes somewhere.

She resumed normal conversation, as if she hadn't sent the cops to the room.

"Guess what?"

"What's up ma?"

"Kaila's getting married. You gotta come home this coming weekend."

Kelis almost fell of the super twin mattress in her room.

"SAY WHAT??!?! Married to WHO?"

"Bobby, who else?"

"Oh, ok. What day?"

As she and her mother went over the travel arrangements, Kelis made a

SO IT DOESN'T HAVE TO BE YOU

mental note to give Cooper a shot, because with Kaila getting married, she didn't have anyone else. Maybe he'd get his act straight. Maybe he could be at least the friend she desired and felt like she deserved.

    Back in NY, Kelis was so excited and sad at the same time. Kaila and Kelis had drawn especially close as Kelis got older, and now her sister was going to start a life of her own. Kelis felt so alone again. She didn't let that stop her from making the programs for the wedding, though. Her sister was happy, so she was happy. And she made all the programs, tied all those stupid bows on them, hid her sister from her groom, went running for umbrellas when it started to rain, decorated the reception area, helped seat guests, and served. She was just happy to see her sister happy, and hoped one day, that maybe just maybe she could be happy. She pondered if she could ever be happy with Cooper, even as friends, and decided he would have to suffice, because she as tired of being hurt.

WHY ME?

Seeing her sister really did something to Kelis. It was almost like she wanted to stay home. There was so much going on that she wasn't a part of, so much she wished she could be there for. And it hurt her to know she wasn't. She was torn between two cities. Her heart was in NY and it was in NC.

As her cousin picked her up from the airport, she chatted with him about life, and he always had something insightful to say. She wished she had him around growing up, because they had become friends during her short time at A&T and he had no problem helping out his "lil cuz" as he called her.

Back at A&T she continued life as normal, which was classes, football games, parties, and Cooper. Unfortunately it wasn't always in that order. She tried to befriend Cooper more, and they continued to get closer.

As she got closer to Cooper, she got farther from God. She never realized that she wasn't praying as much, or really even communicating with God. Dealing with this little boy in a grown

SO IT DOESN'T HAVE TO BE YOU

man's body had taken her away from the most important thing in her life; her relationship with the God that she had grown to understand and respect.

Although God took Randy, in time Kelis understood why. She didn't always get the whole logic and reasoning, but she understood there was a reason for everything. She knew that it didn't kill her not to have Randy around, and she knew that because of him she had a lot more fight in her than she did before knowing him. She also knew that she had goals, and things she wanted to achieve to make him proud. He wasn't her biological father, but he was the only one she ever knew.

She had learned to love and trust God again. Their relationship was tight. When she got to school it was tight. When she met Cooper, it was tight. The more time she spent with Cooper, the looser the relationship got, to the point where Kelis was spiritually unrecognizable. She had gone so far from God that she no longer could hear or feel Him like she used to. She was desolate, and alone. She was being

WHY ME?

attacked by spirits of loneliness and depression, and people began to tell her that if she didn't do something, Cooper would leave her.

Cooper wasn't helping either. He claimed that it was okay when you loved the person. That he wanted to be with her forever and ever and that made it okay. That he felt like he could make her happy, but she wouldn't let him. So, depressed, saddened, oppressed, lonely, and afraid that she'd lose what she was convinced was the only man in the world left that she had that loved her, Kelis wasn't exactly in her right mind when she succumbed to his games and gave herself to him.

Dirty, filthy, nasty… those words filled Kelis' mind as she walked through campus. She felt like everyone knew she had sex with Cooper. She tried to convince herself that it wasn't that bad, and prayed for God's forgiveness in the shower as she scrubbed her body, trying to become clean again, not realizing her virginity was gone, and she'd never get it back.

SO IT DOESN'T HAVE TO BE YOU

Kelis lost a piece of her soul that day that she would end up fighting for. Never knowing about soul ties, she didn't understand the true meaning of the loss of her virginity. Plenty of people had told her not to do anything, they had warned her, and she didn't listen, because she didn't really understand. Experience is an awesome teacher, because she would have given everything she had to get that piece of herself back.

Cooper of course, was completely and totally content with the entire situation. He had gotten the virgin church girl to lay down everything she believed in and succumb to him. His trophy, that's what Kelis was. Of course she didn't realize it then. All she was worried about was how was God ever going to forgive her, and how was she going to tell her mother she made the dumbest mistake of her life and couldn't get it back. She had broken a promise to her mother, to her family, and to God. And she couldn't deal with it. So she swept it under the rug.

WHY ME?

SO IT DOESN'T HAVE TO BE YOU

Chapter 6

In the days to follow, Cooper rationalized sex with her, because she had decided she didn't want to do it anymore. He explained that since they had already done it, it didn't matter that they kept doing it. And she rationalized it within herself, and continued to do it to keep Cooper around. Time passed and she didn't cry as much after they had sex, but it was still painful for her, because somewhere deep inside, something was screaming that it was wrong, and he was wrong, and everything was wrong. And Kelis tried hard to shut that up. It never worked.

Right before thanksgiving break, the first layer of hell broke open for Kelis. Cooper's ex had come back on the scene, and the woman was in fact pregnant. Kelis decided one night she'd stay on campus and hang out with KP. She and KP had a sleepover and talked about everything from Cooper, to

WHY ME?

missing home, to trying to hang out more. She kept certain things about Cooper to herself, and just listened to KP talk about her own life. That night, she had a gut instinct that Cooper was doing something he had no business doing and tried to call him, to no avail. She slept heavy that night.

The next day, she awoke, hung out with KP a little more, and went back to her own room. She logged onto her chat client. She got a message from Cooper. "We need to talk". She knew it was something serious, and was not happy about having to talk to him.

Cooper picked her up. He drove for a while in silence and she just stared at him. In his apartment, she sat on the couch and stared at him some more. He opened his mouth and out spilled what she didn't want to know. "And so I slept with her. But-"Kelis stood up and pushed him and headed for the door. At the door an argument ensues. He starts with the crap.

"Kelis, we are not together!"

SO IT DOESN'T HAVE TO BE YOU

"I understand that but you're not going to be doing whatever the hell you wanna do because we're 'not together'. You have no respect for me and I swear I'm tired of you already."

"I don't understand what your problem is. We are not together! "

Slap. That came from Kelis. A few more slaps. Also from Kelis. Then she broke out into a barrage of punches in his chest that knocked him back. And then she started shrieking.

"You keep telling me things I already know! We're not together, so that makes it absolutely ok for you to sleep with whoever you wanna sleep with! You say you care for me, want to be with me, and the only person in the way of that is you! You're such an actor and I cannot believe I got caught up in this nonsense. I just wanna get away from you."

After a thought she added, "And I bet that baby is yours. That's why you're acting so stupid towards me, because you're about to get all caught up in your

WHY ME?

lie and you weren't expecting that to happen."

He looked into her eyes. "That baby is not mine. I swear to you it's not. I do want you. I need you in my life." He started to cry. "I need you. Be with me, don't leave me. Be my girlfriend" he begged. And since she had never seen anyone do that before, again, she believed him. Stupidity at it's finest. Love is blind, and Kelis was blinded by good acting and physical cover-ups for a much bigger problem.

She went home and enjoyed the holidays with her family. Christmas was awesome and everyone seemed to be enjoying themselves. With all the hell Cooper had put her through; she needed to be around her family. In all actuality, Kelis wanted to stay with her family and didn't want to return to A&T in January. She felt as if she wasn't ready to be on her own. She missed her family. Yet every time she tried to say something, the words wouldn't come out. So in January, Kelis begrudgingly went back to the bondage of being

SO IT DOESN'T HAVE TO BE YOU

alone and afraid, in a world where she had been forced to let go of her will, and give it to someone who didn't know what they were doing. She was starting to hate Cooper, but she couldn't find a way out.

He had become her life. She had nothing and he had everything. She was all alone in his world. She had met one of his brothers and some of his friends. After a while, he finally told her the baby "might" be his. But the woman was such a whore that it could be anyone's baby.

Kelis was in too deep to run while she still had a chance. Stupidly, she "stood by her man". Stupid. Really dumb idea. He claimed that when the baby came, testing was going to be done, and then they could be happy because it's not his. His own mother claimed to believe the baby wasn't his, and that the baby's feet would tell if she was in his bloodline. Kelis believed, because what reason would his mother have to lie.

Roxy's baby had mysteriously disappeared in November and Cooper was no longer speaking to her. Kelis

WHY ME?

found it to be weird, but you never know. Sometimes when people are in pain, they don't feel like talking, and she felt the girl didn't have to explain herself. It was a small detail that didn't make much difference. The problems started for Kelis, in February, where she found herself in a situation she didn't want to be in. Pregnant, and really unhappy about it.

What was the worst part? Cooper was happy about it, beyond chipper. Kelis was a brand new 17 and Cooper was acting like it was the best thing since Yoo-Hoo, because the woman he was "in love" with and wanted to marry was having his child. He told basically everyone, and Kelis began to get settled with it. Abortion was not an option for her, so she did the best she could, to help this secret life growing inside her thrive. A few of her friends new, and they had her back and tried to keep her healthy and calm, but as always, Cooper had to have his circus going on.

The same month she found out about the baby, she found out that a

SO IT DOESN'T HAVE TO BE YOU

mutual friend had made out with Chris while she was gone, and he slept with two coworkers. He tried to apologize and keep her from trying to kill him, but she was so hurt. Then, he lost his job and apartment, and started to move back home with his mom. Kelis was very upset because he had alienated her from every friend she had, and now he was preparing to leave. He informed her that he wouldn't be leaving until after the Spring break. That kept Kelis quiet.

She spent more and more time on campus, sick and in pain, but trying not to tell anyone else about the life that kept her awake at night, which was nicknamed owl, for the times of night she was up sick and uncomfortable and severely depressed.

In the days that followed, Kelis learned to love the life dwelling within her. She talked to her baby, sang to her baby and made future plans to make life better for her child. Kelis, unprepared and afraid, went on survival mode, not for herself, but for the life that had a right to be alive, whether or not she was prepared.

WHY ME?

She went home for Spring break. As much as she wanted to tell her family, she couldn't. She had nobody to confide in, and even if she did, she wasn't sure she wanted to. She just tried to act normal, and it seemed to pass off to everyone. They were just happy to see her. In her time away, she spoke to Cooper's ex, who found out about her pregnancy, and seemed to want to help. His ex provided her with phone numbers, counseling, information about being pregnant, how to deal with doing it alone (Cooper was "happy" but showed no real interest in the welfare of this child), and figuring out the best way to care for your child without outside assistance. She really was very nice, not anywhere near what Cooper made her out to be, and she and Kelis almost became like friends.

Kelis came back to NC, and immediately went to work helping Cooper start the clean on his house. What he didn't know is that she knew he had cheated, and was waiting for him to admit it. What she didn't know is who he had cheated with. So she waited.

SO IT DOESN'T HAVE TO BE YOU

And he never said anything to her. She continued on with life as normal, getting accustomed to the thought of being someone's mother... "Mother" she thought to herself. And then she thought about how Cooper was starting to act, versus her own father. And so Kelis prayed. "Dear Lord, I know we don't talk like we use to, and I'm sorry for that. I don't know what happened, but I need you, Lord. I don't want Cooper to be like my father. Please don't let my baby have to become a product of his environment, because two people screwed up. Use this situation as a conduit for your glory and your honor. In Jesus' name, Amen".

And it seems like clockwork, within the next few days, there was a message posted on the HBCU board Cooper administrated by his ex's best friend. She was talking about how much of a dog Cooper was for cheating on Kelis, and how he lies to her.

Kelis' mind went back to the day that she found women's underwear,

WHY ME?

shaving cream, razors, and head wraps in Cooper's apartment. And when she confronted him, he had played it off as if there was some issue and his brother had a woman in his apartment. "He has my keys, don't trip out, just stay calm" and so she did. This message online was too much.

And then, here comes the woman, the ex. "Apologizing". "I love him" she told Kelis. "Those are my things there. Everything's clean, so you don't have to worry about that. But yeah, while you were gone we were together, and he took care of me, the way he was supposed to. He told me he was excited about our baby, and he was going to be with me."

The tears came slow and hot, escaping painfully from Kelis' eyes. He did it again, he cheated and lied. And so she did what she always did, and she called him.

And he admitted it. He had not only cheated with her, but with another coworker, claiming to not want any of the voodoo she practiced to affect Kelis

SO IT DOESN'T HAVE TO BE YOU

and their baby. He said he loved their baby, that she and the baby were the most important things in his life. And Kelis broke. She fought him, like she wanted to kill him that night. She wrapped her hands around his neck and started to choke him, and he was wriggling away from her. She took a combination of slaps, punches, screams, kicks, and inflicted pain into him. She wanted him to die that night, and not a minute later. She went to the kitchen and grabbed the knife that did the most damage and threw it at his head, and for the first time in her life, her precision failed her. She missed. So she went to grab another one, and was overcome by grief. She dropped to the floor and he came and wrapped his arms around her. "No, don't kill yourself" he pleaded, "I love you and I need you. You can't leave me. I love you. I don't know why I can't do anything right, but it's you I need, I always needed you."

He was lying and she knew it. He liked having her like this, where she couldn't function. She couldn't breathe, and she felt like her life was flashing

WHY ME?

before her eyes. She remembered her mother telling her "nothing ever beats a fail but a try" and "no matter what I love you" and she felt strength return to her.

She got up and pulled herself together as best she could. She went back to her room, and thought of how she would explain this to her family, how it would be, and how God would fix this all.

She never thought of what was to come, she was never prepared. And when it happened, she was twice as alone, right where the enemy needed her to be, to snuff her life out.

SO IT DOESN'T HAVE TO BE YOU

Chapter 7

Kelis didn't want to eat, but she forced it. It wasn't about her at all; she just didn't want any harm to come to her baby. And so she did the best she could to keep him safe. She declared love to the unborn child every day, because even though she herself felt she had nobody, there was no reason for this child to suffer because of it.

And one day, Kelis felt pain. Her stomach felt like it was being ripped apart from the insides. She was shaking slightly and was sweating profusely. She had no idea what was wrong. Her stomach felt as if it was tearing, and the pain was almost unbearable. She began to pray for her safety and for the Lord's healing power and the pain subsided. She thanked God for His blessings and decided to go and get something to eat.

In the cafeteria, she silently went from place to place, making something to eat. And then her eyes grew dim, and the voices seemed distant. She heard

WHY ME?

her friend scream her name, and she hit the floor. She heard the voices around her.

"She's dead weight." Said one boy.

"Kelis, come on sweetie, get up, get up", said a friend of hers.

She heard the security calling the ambulance, and they came swiftly. They got her downstairs and asked her if she was pregnant and she gave them a knowing look.

In the hospital, they couldn't find her veins, and called in the I.V. team. They were starting to worry they weren't going to get any fluids in her. They finally got the I.V. in and started testing her. The nurse sat next to her and kept stroking her hand "I'm sorry sweetheart, I'm sorry. You'll be alright" the nurse tried to soothe her. Kelis already knew there was no going back; there was no saving her baby. And she just had to wait.

SO IT DOESN'T HAVE TO BE YOU

Cooper ended up driving to come see her, and she refused to talk to him about it. After finding that her baby was dead, the doctor decided to perform a scan on her head, to make sure she was alright, and Cooper was confused. Kelis just looked at him. And she thought about how if she had never met him, she would have never ended up in this situation. That if she had just listened, she wouldn't be hurting. Cooper dropped her off, and left her to her pain.

In the next days, more pain came. Pain like Kelis had never felt in her life. Alone, in her room, her baby, her angel, left her. She knew it would happen, but had no idea it would hurt her this bad. Physically, her entire body was hurting her, mentally, she felt guilty, and emotionally she was depressed. And she wanted to die. She started receiving messages from Cooper's ex about how sorry she was. Kelis was so hurt. This woman was pouring salt in her wounds. And so, for the rest of the school semester, Kelis was too depressed to go anywhere, do anything,

WHY ME?

and talk to anybody. And she was ok with it.

Cooper tried to make things better, but the whole time he was sleeping with his ex, and Kelis knew it, but after losing her child, and feeling like she had nothing and no one, she struggled to keep Cooper around. She knew how important having a baby was to him, and she knew that if she seemed completely defective, he would leave her. She was caught, and lost. There was nobody to save her. Nobody would come to rescue her this time. The people that should have loved her weren't around, her baby was gone, the only real father she ever knew was gone, and her boyfriend had never loved her in the first place. And in that room that night, Kelis gave up her will. She prayed to God that she wouldn't wake up. And she prayed that every night. Relief never came.

Cooper had become the model parent to the daughter he now claimed. When she was born, he went to be with her. He told Kelis it wouldn't affect their

SO IT DOESN'T HAVE TO BE YOU

relationship and that he still loved her.

Kelis didn't believe a word that came out of his mouth. She just kept silently wishing to be dead. Nobody understood that she was depressed; everyone was too caught up in the hoopla to understand.

He was gone. The baby she wasn't ready for, but had accepted. When that baby died, a piece of Kelis died. Her fight, her will, her ability to be happy, her overachieving personality, all of it died that night. Cooper was too caught up in his daughter to notice or care, and all of her friends had their lives to tend to.

In a time of insurmountable pain and depression, cooper's ex sent her a message. Now, the once friendly and helpful woman became bitter and vindictive due to Cooper's unhappiness about their baby, said to Kelis "You'll never be able to keep him. You have no ties to him, and let's face it, what I've got, you can't carry", taking digs at Kelis' baby. She wanted to hurt the woman so bad, but couldn't. She had her own problems to deal with. And Kelis started

WHY ME?

to prepare for the journey home. Empty, depressed, unhappy, and lost, she journeyed back to NY.

SO IT DOESN'T HAVE TO BE YOU

Chapter 8

Back in NY, Kelis tried to keep her life as normal as possible. She didn't share much about school, and was depressed about everything.

Her brother got married when she got back from school, and Kelis was so disconnected that she kind of existed through everything.

A day came that she never thought would come.

The day where the "love of her life" would slander her.

On the computer, she saw that he had blogged. In this blog he denied her pregnancy, denied their baby, and accused her of being some sort of con artist.

As she read the blog, she could not believe that he would lie that way. Then she realized that he had gotten back together with his ex. And in order

WHY ME?

for things to look good, he had to deny everything, say Kelis knew about her.

Kelis cried in her room that day. All day long she cried. Cried because her child only mattered to her. She cried because she couldn't tell anyone. She cried because he was unapologetic about their child's death. She screamed because he lied, and made it seem like this child never existed. She cried because she wouldn't be with her baby. Cried because she was with her family and was still all alone.

To Kelis, life was over. There was nothing to look forward to. He was saying underneath the table that he loved her and needed her, but up top he was claiming she was just an excellent liar. He was the liar. He had tricked her into actually believing in his love for her.

And just that fast she flashed back to her baby and went through her life. And she realized Cooper was the father she never wanted her baby to have. Kelis' father had denied her since before she was born. He also fed both parties lies to make himself look better.

SO IT DOESN'T HAVE TO BE YOU

He never apologized to her mother for the hell he put her through, he never apologized to Kelis for helping her hate a part of herself, to the point where she searched for love, in the wrong places, with Cooper.

Cooper used her, and abandoned her. He said that she was his forever, and there would never be anyone like her in his life. That he loved her completely and totally. More lies. Kelis was starting to hate Cooper again, who had two or more very elaborate stories going on. To her, he was saying that their baby was his everything, and he missed her so much that he couldn't listen to her favorite musician, John Legend, without crying. He tried to keep his composure around his daughter's mother because he didn't want her to get more upset.

He was telling the blog site that Kelis was a liar and that he hated her. That he doesn't understand why she lied. He pulled various "sources" to blow the cover off a story that was airtight. Kelis didn't fight. She just struggled to want to stay alive. The pain was eating

WHY ME?

at her. The pain of going through her life without guidance and direction was killing her. The pain of knowing that her angel baby only had one person to care about him, when he deserved two made her bitter. Knowing that Cooper was lying to everyone to keep them on his side made Kelis want to hurt him. She began to wish she had never met Cooper.

It hurt her to think that a child would have been brought into a situation where his father didn't want him. She hated the fact that she almost brought a child into a situation much like hers. She didn't understand how fathers could be so detached, could just forget about the child they helped create. For Cooper it was easy, he had this little girl, that quickly became the apple of his eye, and Kelis became the other woman, although secretly she always had been.

Depression overtook Kelis and became her life. She tried to hold on to the fact that God still loved her, but if her own biological father didn't love her, maybe it was because her Creator didn't

SO IT DOESN'T HAVE TO BE YOU

either? Kelis was set in the fact that God hated her, and placed her on this Earth to make other people's lives easier. Nobody understood her, nobody cared to understand, and God wasn't making things easier.

As time went on Kelis tried to figure out why God would give her this life. "Why God?" she cried in church one morning. She was tired of pain, she was tired of depression, and she was tired of praying for death and death never coming. She had decided she needed to get to the bottom of her situation. She started by writing her baby a letter.

To my unborn child,
    You have NO IDEA how much I miss you, nor how many times I think about you in a day. Right now, the grief is terrible. When u left, I felt like a piece of myself died. You were SO special to me, and to daddy too, and we feel so unhappy now that you are gone. I know they say things happen for a reason, but I feel almost like I was cheated by not still having you here. There are so many times where I am just still, and I will think of how much u changed me with

WHY ME?

your short time of living inside me. You taught me so much by just being there. I learned that there is more to life than just me and daddy, and that the strongest people in the world, are mothers who lost their children. I try HARD not to let the grief overtake me, but you were THAT special, THAT important in my life. I must admit that everyday it gets easier to accept that you are gone, but it doesn't mean I love you any less. I HAVE to learn to let it hurt and to let myself grieve you, or I will be no good to your future brothers or sisters. Some people want me to get over it, but you don't ever have to worry about that, for mommy shall NEVER forget you. You were a MAJOR part of my life, and made me think about someone other than myself, and I love you so much. There is so much I had planned for you, and so much I had in store, but I guess it just wasn't meant to be. Just know that your memory is etched into my heart, and daddy's heart, for the rest of our lives, and know that the major thing u taught ME that I will never forget is that love for your child should be unconditional, and that is

SO IT DOESN'T HAVE TO BE YOU

what me and daddy's love is for you, UNCONDITIONAL.

Love, Mom

    Kelis always felt the need to overcompensate for Cooper's inability to say anything to or about the baby, so she included him in her feelings, more for her own benefit. She never really did know how he felt, because publicly he denied the baby, and privately he never mentioned him, he only mentioned "trying again". Kelis didn't wanna try again. She wanted that baby back. The one she carried as a result of screwing up her life dealing with Cooper. She wanted to watch him grow up and become great. Cooper took that away from Kelis and she hated him for it.

    She remembers her mother's overcompensation for her life. All her life, Kelis could remember Gwyneth trying to find ways to give her more love, let her know that she loved her, but It never was enough. It didn't compensate for her father. Kelis needed her father to love her, and she needed him to show

WHY ME?

that to her. She could not believe she went out looking for someone to provide the love her father never gave, and fell in love with Cooper. Cooper was her father, not because he didn't love her, but because he didn't love their baby. He was a drama king, and she hated him.

In her room that day, she really let herself go. She screamed, yelled, cursed, broke things, and smashed stuff. All in the avenging of her child that deserved to be loved. In the air she screamed "He's gone! It's your fault he's gone! You don't care! You never loved him! You never loved me! You used me! I hate you! You'll never understand!"

And she was right. Nobody would ever understand. She was his mother and nobody else. She screamed and let out the pain and sorrow. She allowed her body to writhe in pain. She let the tears flow, and allowed everything bottled up to come out. That child had become her sunshine, and every day was cloudy without him.

SO IT DOESN'T HAVE TO BE YOU

Her baby was gone, never to return and she didn't want to deal with that. She didn't want to commit to the fact that angels never return. That she wouldn't ever see a physical manifestation of the life she held within her. And she continued to cry. She didn't want to face the music. She didn't know how to cope and wasn't trying to. She just wanted her baby back, and realizing he was never coming back, hurt her. What hurt her more was that Cooper didn't care.

In days, months, even years to come, even though he was with his daughter's mother, he still tried to be with Kelis. It got down to the point where he was still paying her phone bill and talking to her at night, Cooper was declaring his love for her on a daily, claiming that he'd leave his child's mother, and come to NY to be with her. He secretly sent her emails, professing his love, but still, on the blog, he claimed to dislike her. Kelis was sure he had multiple personalities.

WHY ME?

One day he told Kelis he had to let her go, because he had ruined her life. Kelis thought "too bad you didn't realize this before you put me through hell". And she cried. Not because he was leaving her, but because she simply hadn't realized how much pain she was in because of this man.

He continued his double life, of saying one thing to her, because he "just couldn't let her go", and telling his blog another.

When Kelis had gone to NC to get the rest of her things, he claimed to want to say something to her, and wished he had because he still needed her. In reality, Cooper didn't need Kelis; he needed the power she gave him. And Kelis was tired of it. Tired of giving herself to people, tired of being used. And in her room, she deleted every email he ever sent, every messenger contact, left anything he was affiliated, with the exception of her blog (which she blocked him from) and made a conscious decision to let God take over her life once again.

SO IT DOESN'T HAVE TO BE YOU

Chapter 9

In her room, random gospel songs played, and she listened to the words. She started to think about the Bible and scriptures poured into her spirit. When she got to "I will never leave you nor forsake you" she started to cry. She realized then, that she had left and forsook God, for a man, She had put her salvation and relationship on the line for something so unimportant to her life. Love. She had no real idea what love was, she just knew it was something she desired. It brought pain to her heart and spirit to think that she betrayed the only one to ever love her completely and wholly, without reservation.

In her bedroom, she listened to a song she never heard much before. It was by Fred Hammond. The lyrics made the tears flow even more, as she was on the brink of her repentance from disobedience and deliverance from depression.

These lyrics spoke to her spirit and revived her:

WHY ME?

"I've lost some joy, I've lost some time
Now it feels like I will lose my mind
Journeyed long and lost my way
And now it feels like I've lost is all I say

Searching here and over there for what
I've lost
Where is it, I don't know
I will find a way

I will find a way to lift up my hands (lift
up my hands)
And I will find a way to worship You Lord
(find a way, I will find a way)
And though my heart is low, I'll find a
way to give You praise
I'll find a way to love You more

I've lost so much down through the
years
It seems that all I find here lately is a
face so full of tears
I search each dark and empty place
The peace I used to know, somehow I
have misplaced

Searching here and over there for the

SO IT DOESN'T HAVE TO BE YOU

things I've lost
I don't have them anymore

I will find a way to lift up my hands (lift up my hands)
And I will find a way to worship You Lord (find a way, I will find a way)
And though my heart is low I'll find a way to give You praise
I'll find a way to love You more

One thing I've not lost is will to move ahead
And I've kept a faith that trust in You Lord
And I find way down within myself, a love for You Lord that overflows
But I know that I can love You more with every loss and though it all

I will find a way to lift up my hands (lift up my hands)
And I will find a way to worship You Lord (find a way, I will find a way)
And though my life is broken, I'll find a way to give You praise
I'll find a way to love You more

I'll find a way

WHY ME?

I know I will, I know I will,
And though my life is broken I'll find a way to give You praise
I will find a way to love, I will find a way to love
I will find a way to love You more "

Alone, she gave her life back to God that night. There was never a more openness in her spirit. She felt strong, for the first time in a long time, and she knew her life was worth living. She knew there was an awesome God in heaven and that He loved her, and with His love, there was nothing that she couldn't face.

She spoke openly to God about her child and how she felt, the pain she endured. And God soothed her spirit. God spoke to her heart and encouraged her. He let her know that she would make it out of the situation she was in, and that He forgave her. He gave her a new outlook, a new perspective, and although she had a lot to do, and much more areas she had to grow in, Kelis

SO IT DOESN'T HAVE TO BE YOU

wanted to. She was no longer afraid of what the future held, because as long as God loved her and had her back, nothing else mattered.

She sat in the room with her mother, and cried and told her as much of the story as she could. Her mother sat and listened. She hugged her daughter and looked at her. Gwyneth had known the whole time something was wrong, but she didn't push Kelis about it. Kelis feared so much what her mother would say, as her opinion was the only one on this Earth that mattered. And Kelis heard the words she never thought she'd hear. "This is life", said Gwyneth, "and I can't live it for you. But I'm your mother and I am here when you need me. And I love you. I don't care what happened. I'll always love you."

Kelis cried in her mother's embrace, because the love she had been seeking all along was right there. God already prepared the love she

WHY ME?

needed, and he placed it all in the mother that He gave her. She didn't "need" a father's love, when she had God her Father in her life. She just had to allow the love he had for her to well up into her soul. And daily she tried. With her faith restored in God, Kelis was ready to repair her life.

In church, she was coming back to life, she was preparing to go back to school, and she was active again. Depression was leaving her and she was starting to feel happy again. She was determined not to let her past dictate her present and future any longer. After all, you can't cry over spilled milk, you can only wipe it up. So she wiped her tears and began the road to recovery.

Life had not always been so kind to Kelis, but it seemed that everyone was preaching about how God uses situations that you put yourself in "to grow you" and make you stronger. Kelis was slowly becoming an example of growth

SO IT DOESN'T HAVE TO BE YOU

On the journey to finding who she was, she found out a lot about who she wasn't. Through the past year Kelis felt like a failure, like it was just lurking around her waiting to see what havoc it could wreak.

Taking her life back from the enemy, Kelis always questioned God about why these things always seemed to happen to her. It seemed like she always bore the brunt, naturally and spiritually, and she just wanted to know why.

WHY ME?

SO IT DOESN'T HAVE TO BE YOU

Chapter 10

"My strength is made perfect in your weakness" Kelis read from the Bible. The more she learned to read it, the better she was encouraged to stay strong in God.

Cooper had tried to re enter her life a few times in the past months, stating that all he needed was her. And Kelis almost fell for it again, but she realized, somewhere in NC was a woman who thought Cooper was being the perfect picture of boyfriend/fiancé and father and their relationship was wonderful.

She had already gotten into it too many times with that woman, as well as Cooper's mother, and Kelis decided she was done. Her other spiritual mother always told her "If you don't wanna be a doormat, then get off the floor". And Kelis was tired of being everyone's doormat, the object of abuse and rage that was hurt because people's love for her thrived on the seat of their emotions.

WHY ME?

Gone was the naïve 16 year old girl who went to college and lived life way too early. Kelis had decided to start to let all those old ideas of what people wanted her to be die, and become who she knew in her heart she always should be.

She went on a forgiveness spree, Cooper, for being an all around jerk and allowing what was clearly the enemy to use him to try and ruin Kelis' life, her father, yes, for the Barbie doll car, but also for jumping up and leaving the family, denying her from conception, treating her differently than he treated Kaila and the others, Randy, for dying and leaving her to fight this world without a father figure to have her back.

Most importantly she forgave herself, for allowing the past to dictate her future. For letting people tell her who to be and trying to be that, Kelis was sorry. She didn't know back then that people would try to live through her, and make her what they wanted to be. She had no idea that not many ever cared what happened to her, and she was

SO IT DOESN'T HAVE TO BE YOU

letting go of the fact that they ever would. She realized that the reason why rappers only thank God and their mom is because the God honest truth is, in most cases, those two are all you can count on.

As she continued to walk through this forgiveness journey, her creativity expanded. She began to create rhythmic expressions of her love for God and vice versa, creating a flow that was just hers. She began to use her body to express her feelings about God via dance, and enjoying the freedom that comes from a God who loves you. She even began to teach at the church again.

Condemnation can keep a person down, Christian or not. And when you know you've done wrong, you feel bad for even trying to tell someone how to do right, but Kelis overcame by knowing that it was different because she was no longer the same. She had been changed into a person who had the capability to love and be loved, to learn to trust again the way she could be

WHY ME?

trusted, and most of all, to be accepted for exactly who she was.

Kelis grew stronger in her faith and after a while discovered that God did in fact talk to her. Prophecy is what they called it, and He really did speak through people. SO Kelis tried to keep an open ear, to let God say what was on His mind.

This was a sign for Kelis that God is real. For a long time, she didn't believe in Him because of Randy, so she had read up on other religions, tried to see what they were about, and understand. Some she did.

What got Kelis back to God was not the fact that her mother was a Pastor. It was that God is the only one who ever answered her back. She was highly critical because after all, did he answer when Randy was dying? Yes, God did.

The problem with most people who try Christianity out was not that God never answered, it was that they didn't like the answer, so they sought Allah,

SO IT DOESN'T HAVE TO BE YOU

Buddha, and Confucius, whoever to get the answer they desired and in most cases, no news is good news. If yes is the answer you want to hear, and God says no, but every other religious authority doesn't answer, you're going to say that God's having an off day, so, boom I'll do it.

Kelis had begun to realize God was talking to her for a long time, and because she wasn't paying attention she never heard a word He said.

One day, Kelis was preparing to leave for church. As she went down the first step in front of her house, she slipped and fell right to the bottom. Her knee was all scraped up and she was a little bruised, but she got up and went to church anyhow.

After Sunday school, everyone was trying to figure out who was doing praise and worship, because nobody "felt like being bothered". So Kelis, normally just the backup soprano said to her mom "I'll do it". And she agreed.

WHY ME?

God visited Kingdom Builders that day and He showed up to heal, not just the people in the audience, but Kelis as well. Having always been in the background, she never desired more than to just be in God's presence, but today she was ushering the congregation in to the glory of God, and they were gaining entry.

Her mother continued to encourage her in that position, until it was something she did almost all the time and it made her feel special to minister to God that way.

In that very same service she could hear her mother prophesying saying "Whatever you need is here, reach up and grab. Whatever you ask will not be denied."

Kelis took that opportunity, and asked God "Why me?" just one more time. He told her to open her eyes and survey the people worshipping. Her eyes fell on all the younger girls at the church who were still growing up. And he said "So it doesn't have to be them."

SO IT DOESN'T HAVE TO BE YOU

Chapter 11

If you had the opportunity to make sure the things that happened to you, wouldn't happen to someone else, because they'd be able to recognize it, this is for you.

If you got all the way through this and realized you don't want to go through the same things Kelis went through, this too is for you.

If you got an understanding of how the enemy sends things to harm you, and you feel a little wiser to the game, this is for you.

The question "Why me" echoed and resonated through me for years. I hated the fact that I was supposed to share this. I abhorred the very mention of me testifying my pain and trials so people can clap because I made it.

I didn't write this for money or fame, I wrote it because I don't want people who have been through any or all of the situations in this book to feel

WHY ME?

like they are alone. I don't want people to continue in a state of unhappiness because nobody understands how these situations affect people. Not just women, men as well.

When God spoke to me and said that it didn't have to be other people, I will admit, I was still in a selfish way, hording what happened to me because it was painful and because I still felt like nobody would understand me. How do you cross over?

By realizing, in 6 years it could have been your sister, because you didn't tell it. By realizing that you're not the only person on this great big Earth who had these issues, and by realizing, nobody is going to tell it like you. Everyone has a voice that needs to be heard, and it needs to be heard so that there aren't a hundred other voices screaming for help from a situation that you overcame.

Today, I'm glad it was me. I wish the person who went through it before me would have said something, but that's fine. I have the vision of helping someone overcome that obstacle. And if it has to be me sharing and bearing all, it's ok.

Vulnerability comes in many stages and this is mine. Allowing myself to be open and to talk about just a small piece of what happened in my lifetime is worth it if ONE person gets help from this.

Whether it's someone like Kelis, or Kaila, Gwyneth, or Kevin doesn't matter to me. If it's someone who realizes they're just like Cooper and they stop what they're doing and grow, that's enough for me.

Even if it's for a little sister who watched it happen and vows not to let it happen to her, because she sees the light, it's fine.

If it's someone who lost their faith in God and realizes maybe it was them so it didn't have to be their daughter or son, and they find their way back to God, I'm all right.

WHY ME?

I realized long ago I'd be subject to other people's judgment of this book and that one day you may read someone else's version, but the fact of the matter is, nobody's telling this better than me, because it was never really me telling it. The Holy Spirit inspires creativity, so it's what He wants to say. To take your life and make it readable takes creativity surpassed by mere physical beings, and I'm glad to be a conduit of creativity.

SO IT DOESN'T HAVE TO BE YOU

Chapter 12

    This portion of my life, based on a true story, with some names changed to keep the peace, is me in a nutshell. And I hope the question has been answered. Just because you read this and it wasn't you doesn't mean you read in vain. Keep in mind how it may help someone else.

    I find freedom in this book and freedom in these words: THIS WAS ME. It's not anymore. I remember her and what she's been through, but I've grown so much in this time. It was hard to try to bring this to a close because it meant it really was over.

    It meant I had to really leave this area in my life, and because I was there for so long, I wondered if I really knew how. I know how today!

WHY ME?

I've said goodbye to the old "Kelis" and embraced the newness that is Blaze. In my secret heart, I knew that this story would not be done justice if I never said who I was, so here I am.

I've fought for months, trying to figure out if it's long enough or too long, if people would understand or if they'd even care.

I learned writing is like Christianity, it's a faith walk. I have faith that whoever needs this, it will fall into their hands and they won't have to write this very same book one day.

I also have faith that someone will be delivered from the shackles and bondage that your mind keeps you in from pain.

I want people to let things go, even as Jesus did.

Above the clouds and behind the veil, I found the ways to close this chapter. Not of this book, but of my life. If I don't take anything else from my experience, I know that God is my

SO IT DOESN'T HAVE TO BE YOU

Father and Jesus is not only my brother, but my friend.

The Bible says that the greatest love is to die for a friend. Jesus died for me so that I could live. I'm sure at one point he asked the same question I did.

He prayed to His Father, same pain in his heart and said "Why Me?" and God quickly answered "So it doesn't have to be them".

WHY ME?

SO IT DOESN'T HAVE TO BE YOU

Epilogue

If you haven't already figured it out, I became an ACTIVE Christian from this experience.

The question "why me" was so pertinent to a part of the deity that I would be crazy to not go there for a minute

A Perfect being, never did anything wrong, died for us. For real. If we all are serious about it, scientists are saying it happened.

The point we're missing is, He died for us. Never had to die, because He never did anything wrong.

Many of our own forefathers would be dead if it wasn't for this one act of love. Do you love anyone enough to die for them?

Most would not die for their own families, let alone nations upon nations, inclusive of those who actually killed you.

WHY ME?

People get caught up in the hype of proving each and every miracle, of finding the exact place Jesus stood on mountaintops to teach. People want to rationalize something that's irrational.

Someone came to die for all of us so that not only could we live here on Earth, but live in Heaven. Someone stopped the chains of bondage the enemy (satan) had on us.

Speaking of satan, let's just bust up some things about him. The devil is not ugly, he's gorgeous. And he comes in more than one form, and it's not any silly plot.

Whatever causes you destruction and or can kill you, it's him. The devil is negativity, frustration, that feeling in the night that scares you, the voice that says nobody loves you. That's him. He's subtle, and he wants you to come live in hell.

Jesus is positivity, He is peace and love. He is forgiveness, He is self control. He is every good and perfect

SO IT DOESN'T HAVE TO BE YOU

thing on this Earth, and He wants you to live, forever, with Him.

Another myth is, in the event we all get to Heaven, we're staying. Not true. After God finishes purging the Earth again, we get to come back here and LIVE our lives. In peace and harmony, the way most people SAY they want to live.

Jesus died so we wouldn't have to. Today I challenge you to choose LIFE. And this is how:

Romans 10:9-10

"That if you confess with your mouth 'Jesus is Lord', and believe in your heart that God raised Him from the dead, you will be saved. For it is with the heart that you believe and are justified, and it is with your mouth that you confess and are saved."

That's all. All God wants is for you to believe that, and receive His love for you, that there's someone who sees into the periscope of time, and wants you to be prosperous and happy!

WHY ME?

Congratulations on finishing this book! It means so much to me that anyone would even care to read it. I hope that you have found something here, even if it wasn't what you were looking for.

I want each and every reader to know that you are fearfully and wonderfully made, and that God LOVES YOU! And that I love you too!

One day I hope to meet some of the people who read this and I pray that every need in your lives be met.

The Bible says that we overcome by the blood of the lamb and by the word of our testimony. The blood was applied when I got saved, and here's my testimony, shared with you all.

I AM AN OVERCOMER!

And so are you.

Peace and Blessings,

Blaze

SO IT DOESN'T HAVE TO BE YOU

Questions for Discussion

1) Do you find yourself in any of these characters? Why?

2) Have you ever found yourself asking the question "Why Me?"

3) In the course of this book, did you recognize any personal misconceptions about people you know?

WHY ME?

SO IT DOESN'T HAVE TO BE YOU

www.ingramcontent.com/pod-product-compliance
Lightning Source LLC
Chambersburg PA
CBHW070452100426
42743CB00010B/1589